The Protection of Ghosts

Natalie Linh Bolderston

V.

Published in the United Kingdom in 2019
by V. Press,
10 Vernon Grove,
Droitwich,
Worcestershire,
WR9 9LQ.

ISBN: 978-1-9165052-3-0

The Protection of Ghosts was selected and guest edited by Carrie Etter as a V. Press Guest
Editor Selection title.

Cover design © Ruth Stacey, 2019.
Printed in the U. K. by Vernon Print & Design, Droitwich, WR9 8QZ.

Acknowledgements

*Thank you to the following publications, where versions of some of these poems first
appeared: Cha: An Asian Literary Journal, L'Éphémère Review, Oxford Poetry, Smoke, The
Good Journal, and Voice & Verse. 'Operation Ranch Hand' received a silver 2018 Creative
Future Literary Award. I am grateful to the following people for their support and inspiration
(poetry-related or otherwise): Trinh Hue Bolderston, Romalyn Ante, Martin Bolderston,
Carrie Etter, Dan Fitt-Palmer, Sarah Goh, Abigail Keay, Sarah Leavesley, Kinneret Livne,
Quang Nguyen, Danielle Poole and Bạch Tuyết Tạ.*

V.

For Mum, Bà Ngoại, and our ancestors

V.

V.

Contents

V.

V.

I watch my mother peel longan fruits –

nails to capillary skin, eyeball flesh,
beetle-stone centre.

I watch, know she is thinking
of a long-ago rooftop,

branches reaching from concrete pots,
pollen fuzzing her summer áo dài.

On the roof, longans taste like sour rain
and street dust. Inside, she rolls them

in salt, chilli, the smell of incense.

                    *

Her mother wipes white pulp
from between her fingers,

carries a bowl of half-peeled fruit
behind a heavy door.

My mother puts her ear to the wall

but only detects the threat of flies,
a mosquito humming on her neck.

                    *

On her way to the black market,
my mother slips a stone from her pocket –

wonders if one day the soldiers will see a green shoot
and suspect she put it there.

The night she leaves smells like sweet rot.
The family drives through back roads

dark as the mouths of dogs. Her mother's hands
fumble with the ghosts of longans.

                    *

I put my head in her lap, close my eyes.
Her chewing nestles in my hair.

She streaks a plasma rainbow above my eye,
licks her fingertips as she
mumbles *không giống, không giống.*

Divinations on Survival

夬 Guài [displacement, parting]

43.

we left rain laced with tiny   gods, slack-skinned sun

like a cooked fruit unravelling across sea. in sagging boats,

we spent nights learning every word for *sorry*, my body

blue with exile. since I learned it is a privilege to love,

every birth feels like a killing. my child arrives in a chokehold –

if only I could still my blood long enough for this to end.

損 Sǔn [diminishing]

41.

49 days since I tasted pork & you left for Saigon.

how hunger coppers my   mouth. has it been

so long since I found my-   self unmothered. I learn

to avoid the last pig I   can't kill. the days

swarm like flies scaling   my stomach. I smoke,

I swallow my name & nothing else when I hear soldiers

家人 Jiā Rén [dwelling people, the family]

37.

to keep you grounded as your mind glides up

I take you to every place you have laughed in,

    lost teeth. as if this   country were still yours

I show you eras you cannot touch in our garden of

    buried bribes. here, we   finger bruises into flowers.

you cry as if you know where I have scattered ashes,

Bà Ngoại

I.

A woman of habits and strong perfume. Still apple-bodied from the swell of twelve pregnancies. Legs that totter without a cane, yet arms that permit spontaneous press-ups. Hair like silver blades of grass, shorn in mourning. Six a.m. – the chanting of monks drifts up the stairs –

Nam Mô A Di Đà Phật,
Nam Mô A Di Đà Phật,
Nam Mô A Di Đà Phật.

on loop until eight. The words would lose all meaning, except I never knew what they meant. I stumble in on her vigil. She hands me a joss stick, a flaming baton. I bow low to Siddhartha and my smoke-and-ashes grandfather. They smile indulgently from gilt frames, as we lay out red grapes, persimmons, winter melon soup.

II.

Big black méo! she cries one day.
We have mice?
No! Grabs, drags me, points. *Méo!*
A fat ink blot of a cat licks its mouth at us.
You know, in England they're good luck.
She shudders, draws the curtains.

III.

Another day, she rolls two brass columns into my palm.
A secret, she explains. Forty pounds in coins. I feel like a pirate.

She winks and stitches away with her crochet hooks. *Now you try.*
I am soon tripping over my loops. She tugs and my blunders unravel. *Again,* she
says.

IV.
Some days, I am more than her infant granddaughter. When I look taller, fuller
she begins to visualise me in red. I know this when she fastens gold around my
wrist. A heart and key dangle from my veins. Dainty. Easily lost. *For when he
asks,* she says.

Typhoon in Xiamen

Trees wrapped in orange smog
will thunder and fall like gods.

Somewhere, a grandmother lights a joss stick,
prays for the protection of ghosts.

A widow counts her teeth,
checks her children's moles and palms
for a sign.

There should be lanterns, mooncake, chrysanthemum tea,
but the other half of our family is marooned
in a high rise across the bridge.

The city is neon-eyed and slavering
as the sky lunges.

*

Decades earlier, my grandfather, fifteen,
studies under some streetlight not far from here.

All the lights in his house are out,
and someone has locked the door.

He looks up, weighs the air in his hands.

Rats run from the shore
as he chases his papers down the street.

*

In the morning, we search for an open café
among the almost-return of taxis and halogen lights.

Vapour presses against my chest.
Soldiers in green and red shirted volunteers

carry wooden bodies on their shoulders,
stew yellow canola flowers underfoot.

Koi

In the old story, many swam
upstream, writhed in sickle bends, slivers
of red-mottled moon.

The waterfall spat most back. One leapt against the gush
of white – in bright air, its body swelled into a rope
of muscle. Fins blossomed with four dragon toes.

Today I see them, chiffon-hemmed lotus petals,
spiralling, chanting bubbles to no one.
I wait for sword-tip faces to spit fire.

Uncle drops rice. Stillborn maggots slip
through the surface of the pond. Heads cluster, beg
with sucker mouths, greedy kisses.

I watch as he conjures piranhas. He looks back.
Much nicer than fish food,
he says. Smiles a moon sliver.

Operation Ranch Hand

Operation Ranch Hand was a codename for a chemical warfare campaign carried out by the US during the Vietnam War.

And just like that, the trees fold around them.
Gas snarls at a woman's shoulders,
presses her belly to dirt.

She does not know about the scar
that is forming inside, that her daughter
will be born wordless on a stretcher.
That she will carry the smell
of dead leaves on her skin,
her name already cremated.

Her house shakes on a stack of bones
as she realises that pain is a man in a mask
who will tread her ribs like a railroad,
string up her arms and call her hunted.
Her sons will search her mouth for a curse,
douse her sores with polluted water
as her breasts leak ash.

Until now, she did not know how easily
the body can disown itself, all cells
unbraided. She will look up to see God
eating his own hands.

Triệu Thị Trinh, or The Lady General Clad in Golden Robe

I learn flight from every wingless thing,
pull the sky down to meet me.

Summer clenches around my womb. I barter
for my child-skin and lose.

I want to believe I was named for my mother,
that I gasped whole from her body, full-tongued

and armoured. I want to believe that I wear her face
to every war, fight with the anger of our failed gods.

I scream from an elephant's head, and women remember
the taste of their teeth. I lead us through mountains,

navigate by moon-spattered blade, measure distance
in bodies and crows. With their eyes closed,

any of these men could be my father. Each one
a felled ox, rain searching for an opening in their chests.

They feed me their ghosts hair by hair, tooth by tooth.
I reach into my body and pull at their bloodless voices

as if they want to be found, as if they saw me and knew
the only way home was to fall.

Oh mother, I have learned so much without you,
so why is every sound a broken wing? Why

do I remember every place I've knelt in prayer,
rinsed blood from my mouth? I want to tell

how it will end: my golden armour
the only body I have left, begging you,

please, don't die without me.

My mother's nightmares

taste like seawater and vomit, handfuls of spat blood. The sky is a paper bruise, and it is always 1978. A gunshot forces her to carry the dead in her womb.

A boy who looks too much like her brother hides in a river. The girl with long twin braids cradles her amputated leg.

Her sister's fingertips on the backs of her hands, soft nose of a boat-rat – its shadow a threat against the wet wood.

The branches of a plum tree become her father's arms, then a zigzag of bones tied together with hair.

She buries her face at the roots of her house, packs her mouth with dirt to remember the taste.

*

I dream that the curtains above me leak flowers into my mouth. I open my chest to let the light in, to see something live. Vines fasten my ribs to the ceiling and pull –

my mother reaches, but cannot keep me on the ground. She grows smaller, our hands cannot touch, and I do not know whether I am rising or she is falling –

There is a garden where her skin is drying on the line, a handful of her hair on the lawn. The flower beds are piles of stones, or caves, hiding things the sun does not want.

Corpse feet, white and windless, carry a red sheet wearing my mother's face
and I do not know whether to hide or run to her blue lips –

*

I come to her in the dark, ask her to show me she's alive, that her hands are
still part of her body. We both know there are some things we can only
consider with our eyes closed.

I watch her on her knees at the shrine, face clenched against continuing.

After, she holds my body like a wreck of wood, traces names on skin. I
imagine what is implied –

Darling, you were fleshed
from a war and a cold block of flats,
but I love you anyway.

She washes the sweat out of our hair.

When Bà Ngoại tells stories

Sometimes, they bristle, snap
at our hands when we try to latch on –

> *With no Buddhism, I would be dead.*
> *All my children in sea.*
> *You see? You see why I need?*

Sometimes they are tuberous,
bloated with other stories, aching
to split their skins –

> *Look! There is new wind in the sky.*
> *When I see, I have to go after.*
> *You like that, even when you small.*

Sometimes, they meiosise at her touch,
come barefoot, soft-boned, lilac-veined –

> *Bà cũng yêu mẹ của bà nhiêu lắm.*
> *I see her sometimes.*

Sometimes, my mother writes them down,
and I fall asleep with them pressed
against my hip. By morning,
they have entered my body –

That day, we wore white pyjamas.
The van came when it was still dark.
I don't know who was driving.

Sometimes I know them already,
tucked away in some suitcase
or wooden box, like children's gloves
or early teeth –

They used to cry when their nannies left.
Every year, I had a new baby under my arm.
I want to go to the floating island today –
reminds me of family.

Often, they smell like lychees, spearmint,
the week-old clementines
we placed beside the shrine –

I remember,
we grew a lot of fruit and greens on the roof.
Always eat with chilli and salt. You try!

Sometimes they have slippery backbones,
feed on seawater and wild pearls –

Your mummy used to bring fish home live
in water. But when one touch her hand,
she dropped the bucket and ran home.

Her eyes are never cataract white,
but dark and fizzing with dancehall hum –

One, two, three, cha-cha-cha.
That is how we did it. Now you.

Sometimes they rupture,
pattern our open palms with dark juice
and stale tears –

July make me scared. All the hungry ghosts
escape. Pray loud! Chase them away.
Pray for your parents.

Sometimes, they are hot and binding,
solder us vein to vein
and rib to rib –

Vì lẽ đó cháu và bà giống nhau. Remember, okay?

Reflection

I.

There was no one coming,
so my mother uncovered her head.

A long time ago,
she was on a bus to Saigon.
Her hair was falling out,

her mother's rings sliding
from her fingers.
They sent her to her uncle,

a pharmacist. They thought
he could make her well.
They could not see how she tried

to love her bones without flesh,
how her body was an arrow
spinning through rain.

How when she said *tôi mạnh,*
she meant *forgive me.*

II.

Years later, she erases
her name from mine.
Asks if I remembered to pinch

my nose that morning,
as if I could exile her
from my face.

She says, *You have big eyes,*
like your daddy.
That makes you beautiful.

She tells me my skin is sore
because I *have too much heat inside.*
We try cucumber, green tea,

Chinese herbs. We try scrubbing and scrubbing.
She remembers how she once wanted
to set fire to her breasts and stomach,

but had no faith in her hands.
How she tied her wrists to the sea,
carved strips from her legs and ribs.

Each night, I leave a kiss on her eyelids,
begin to stitch her skin over mine.

Jingwei

In Chinese mythology, Jingwei is a bird reborn from the Emperor's daughter, who drowned in the Eastern Sea. She drops twigs and pebbles into the water, trying to fill it up so no one else will die as she did.

To cup this sound in my throat
like a name that isn't mine.

To sweat like a pressed petal,
eat from the ground with my hands.

To recognise clouds as faces
of drowned women:
I was born to lose this body.

To wage war with mineral claws,
crush foam into white blossoms.

To count the pricks in my skin,
accept my underskirt of feathers.

To hollow my bones to sticks
and wait to be woken.

Hạ Long Bay

Sun has burned a hole
in the grey veil of sky.
Half-disguised by trees,
the mountain glowers,
remembers everything.

We slip through the valley
in a green canoe
rowed by a young man –
striped shirt, muscled shoulders.

Mangroves lean in,
knotted to the rockface
with swollen roots –

their rings, I think,
as many as our fingerprints.
A black kite springs alive
from the mist,
its call in my throat.

Below, sea snakes
ropes of liquorice.
A slight turn,
a flash of green water –

a village floating
on plank-and-barrel rafts.
Faces look out
from tin doorways.
Children wave
from wicker coracles
like upturned shields.

*

At 5 a.m., when the sky
is still purple,
we float to the market –
wooden boats and buckets
of fruit. We eat lychees
in the half-light.

When storms come
all will be evacuated.
It is hard to live in battle
with typhoons, monsoons,
although – as my grandmother says –
this is the land
taking a breath.

Questions for My Mother

I ask her how it felt to leave the house that pierced the sky-ceiling. I ask who they trusted to take care of the pigs; if they knew how to slaughter them properly; if she knew she was never coming back. I ask how much her father minded when she married a white man; why she wailed when she saw I had her nose.

i.

Your first patient of the day asks for tea. When
your hands touch, her skin is like tissue paper.
Her arms are bruises and needle pricks.

He – her son? – stops you. He asks for tea
that you cannot give. The rules, you explain.
He shows his teeth. *Go back to China.* You are not from China.
Go back to wherever you came from.
You have nowhere to go back to.

STATELESS, stamped on your papers,
and the words repeat: *GoBackGoBackGoBack.*

ii.

The man with the biro behind his ear teaches you shame.
You cannot answer his questions. He slaps the desk,
asks again, slower, wider. You can see his tonsils.
There is a silence as long as the distance home –
GoBackGoBackGoBack. He doesn't need to say it.

Your tongue, that heavy plush, refuses to bend.

He strings up your vocabulary in front of you:
words he does not know, or want. You watch them wither
on the windowsill while he points, repeats.

iii.

You wonder whether anyone would have wanted you more
if you were your photograph: sixteen, red-lipped, pale-skinned,
yellow-bloused, a *Miss Saigon* dream.

Do they not see that you are beautiful
in nurse's blue, hands chapped and muscular from days
of bedbaths and tourniquets?

iv.

These days, you pick up a book, bathe in verbs,
wash the sun off your shoulders. Snow falls
on your flip-flopped feet when you walk to class.
You wonder if you will miss

the chill if you ever go back – is it still home?
Or the place that chased you out?

She tells. She tells of upturned drawers, white pyjamas. Buying baby milk on the black market, because she was sorry her youngest sisters were born on the smoking tail of their wealth. Her father's cigarettes, his shaking fingers, the South's president showing apologetic palms on TV. Stealing strawberries on the way home from school, before she ever needed to. Lining their clothes with the family gold and hoping no one would notice their heavy walk. A white van, a brown bag. A boat, already cracking with a warning: *GoBackGoBackGoBack.*

From Bà Cố to Bà Ngoại

Daughter, do not let your feet grow septic with running,
your tongue surrender in your throat.

The country will not know your name.
When your children forget my name, remind them:
I am not just someone who used to love you.

Because you share my bed in times of sickness
and pregnancy, reach for me
as the sun paints you awake.

Con yêu của mẹ, can you hear me?
Remember this when you cradle your daughter
in the early hours, and you want
to throw prayers at the walls
and set the bedposts alight.

Instead, send me a picture of a little girl with frost in her hair
and a face that used to be yours.

When you return from the cold,
show me the shape of the water you crossed,
the blue air in your lungs.

Aubade

Let the first joss sticks of the day burn slowly
between your palms. Plant them like reeds in ash

as smoke scars his photograph. Feel his name stretch out
behind the buzz of the cassette tape.

Let daylight interrupt,
paint the walls with watery prisms

that catch in the folds of your orange áo dài.
Shed them with a twirl, fistfuls of cabbage whites.

Let your daughters cook sticky rice, egg rolls, soup,
thirteen cups of jasmine. Notice how they look less alike these days:

some lipsticked, grey-flecked, others ageless. See the chrysanthemums,
lilies, wild roses awaken at their silk skirts, the gold peeking

from beneath their sleeves. See the eldest two holding hands
and shopping bags. Let them smash the pink skull of a pomegranate, scrape

seeds into white bowls. Let red candlewax drip
onto the persimmon tower, melted sunrise.

Let your sons light their Chinese cigarettes, open the rice wine
that knocked them sideways when they were young.

Let the children call you Bà Ngoại, absorb your giggle, toothy smile,
your Chanel No.5. Let them ask, who is Ông Ngoại,

and why don't we remember him? (Let someone else answer.)
Let them dive into the pillows and folded sheets, run lilacs and yellows

through their fingers. Let them swing from the doorframes,
not knowing what has passed.

Sit too far away, let yourself be pulled back. Surrender to a bowl,
a fork, accept that curtains will part. Forgive winter for coming

too early, its tail in the air before you unearthed the blankets, sweaters,
bedsocks – substitutes for a body beside a body. When you lie back,

listen for the brag of the tape, his static-filled cough, the rustle
of his yellow shirts, pressed like last year's daffodils.

V.

Notes

Glossary

Áo dài – Vietnamese national dress
Bà Cố – great grandmother
Bà cũng yêu mẹ của bà nhiêu lắm – I loved my mummy very much too
Bà Ngoại – maternal grandmother
Con yêu của mẹ – my darling daughter
Không giống – not the same as before
Nam Mô A Di Đà Phật – a Buddhist chant
Ông Ngoại – maternal grandfather
Tôi mạnh – I'm strong/I'm fine
Vì lẽ đó cháu và bà giống nhau – that is why you and me are the same

'Divinations on Survival' uses a form invented by Kristin Chang, called the I-Ching. This is named after a Chinese method of divination. Each stanza takes the shape of an I-Ching hexagram, and can be read left to right starting with the first line, or left to right starting with the last line. The stanza titles and numbers are also the names and numbers of the hexagrams.

V.

Natalie Linh Bolderston studied English at the University of Liverpool, where she won the 2016 Felicia Hemans Prize for Lyrical Poetry and the 2017 Miriam Allott Poetry Prize. She now works as an editorial assistant. Her work has been featured in *Cha: An Asian Literary Journal*, *L'Éphémère Review*, *Oxford Poetry*, *Smoke*, *The Good Journal*, *The Tangerine,* and *Voice & Verse*. In 2018, she received the silver Creative Future Literary Award, was awarded second place in the Timothy Corsellis Poetry Prize, and was commended in the Young Poets Network's prose poetry competition.

V.